WORLD'S DEADLIEST

VOLUME 2

JOSHUA WILLIAMSON
WRITER

**NICK DERINGTON, CLAYTON HENRY, MAX RAYNOR,
GLEB MELNIKOV, DALE EAGLESHAM, ANDREI BRESSAN**
ARTISTS

DAVE McCAIG, ALEJANDRO SÁNCHEZ
COLORISTS

JOHN J. HILL
LETTERER

DAVID MARQUEZ and **ALEJANDRO SÁNCHEZ**
COLLECTION COVER ARTISTS

BATMAN CREATED BY BOB KANE WITH BILL FINGER
SUPERMAN CREATED BY JERRY SIEGEL AND JOE SHUSTER
SUPERBOY CREATED BY JERRY SIEGEL
BY SPECIAL ARRANGEMENT WITH THE JERRY SIEGEL FAMILY

PAUL KAMINSKI Editor – Original Series & Collected Edition
BEN MEARES Assistant Editor – Original Series
STEVE COOK Design Director – Books
DAMIAN RYLAND Publication Design
ERIN VANOVER Publication Production

MARIE JAVINS Editor-in-Chief, DC Comics

DANIEL CHERRY III Senior VP – General Manager
JIM LEE Publisher & Chief Creative Officer
JOEN CHOE VP – Global Brand & Creative Services
DON FALLETTI VP – Manufacturing Operations & Workflow Management
LAWRENCE GANEM VP – Talent Services
ALISON GILL Senior VP – Manufacturing & Operations
NICK J. NAPOLITANO VP – Manufacturing Administration & Design
NANCY SPEARS VP – Revenue

BATMAN/SUPERMAN VOL. 2: WORLD'S DEADLIEST

DC Comics, 2900 West Alameda Ave., Burbank, CA 91505
Printed by LSC Communications, Owensville, MO, USA. 9/17/21. First Printing.
ISBN: 978-1-77950-920-8

Library of Congress Cataloging-in-Publication Data is available.

BATMAN/SUPERMAN #7

cover by
NICK DERINGTON

KANDOR.

A SHINING BEACON OF KRYPTONIAN KNOWLEDGE AND CULTURE. OUR GREATEST MINDS CALLED IT HOME.

MY FATHER MET MY MOTHER THERE.

WHEN BRAINIAC STOLE KRYPTON, SHRANK IT DOWN AND BOTTLED IT...

...IT BROKE MY PARENTS' HEARTS.

IT WAS A BITTERSWEET FATE, FOR ITS IMPRISONMENT WAS ALSO ITS PROTECTION, SAVING IT FROM KRYPTON'S DESTRUCTION.

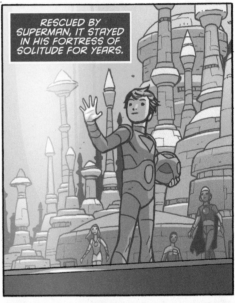

RESCUED BY SUPERMAN, IT STAYED IN HIS FORTRESS OF SOLITUDE FOR YEARS.

I UNDERSTAND THAT OVER TIME, THE CITIZENS OF KANDOR LEARNED TO LIVE A LIFE OF PEACE WITHIN THEIR ENTRAPMENT...

...UNTIL ROGOL ZAAR.

ANOTHER WORLD LOST BECAUSE THE HOUSE OF EL COULD NOT DO WHAT NEEDED TO BE DONE.*

WHEN I CLOSE MY EYES...

*SEE THE **MAN OF STEEL** *GRAPHIC NOVEL FOR THE FULL STORY. --PAUL*

...I CAN HEAR THEIR SCREAMS.

NO MORE.

NOW THAT I, AT LONG LAST, HAVE A WORLD TO BUILD...

...KANDOR CAN BE PROPERLY... AVENGED.

BOOM

IT'S THE LITTLE THINGS THAT GET TO YOU.

BRUCE SAYS HE CAN SOMETIMES STILL SMELL HIS MOTHER'S PERFUME IN THE MANSION.

AND I GET THAT. REALLY, I DO. SOMETIMES WE GET SO WRAPPED UP IN THESE BATTLES WE FACE, OUR MEMORIES BECOME *GHOSTS*. THEY HAUNT US IN WAYS WE DON'T *EXPECT*.

EVERY DAY, I LOOK AT THIS SYMBOL ON MY CHEST AND I'M REMINDED OF MY WORLD.

BOTH OUR STORIES START THE SAME.

WITH LOSS.

AND WE BOTH DEAL WITH IT IN THE SAME WAY.

WE KEEP OURSELVES BUSY.

SO THE *GHOSTS* NEVER *CATCH* US.

...HOW EASY IT IS TO BELIEVE *YOU* ARE THE HERO OF YOUR STORY...

I ALWAYS DREAD COMING HERE...

JOSHUA WILLIAMSON writer
NICK DERINGTON artist

DAVE McCAIG colorist **JOHN J. HILL** letterer
NICK DERINGTON cover
ANDY KUBERT & BRAD ANDERSON variant cover
BEN MEARES assistant editor **PAUL KAMINSKI** editor
BEN ABERNATHY group editor
SUPERMAN created by **JERRY SIEGEL** and **JOE SHUSTER**.
By special arrangement with the **JERRY SIEGEL FAMILY**.
BATMAN created by **BOB KANE** with **BILL FINGER**.

STRYKER'S ISLAND.

...SO MANY PEOPLE I WISH WE COULD HAVE SAVED...

STRYKER'S ISN'T A NORMAL PRISON, SUPERMAN...

...AND NEITHER IS ITS *GRAVEYARD.*

THE DATABASE WE'VE BEEN BUILDING HAS BEEN *WORKING.* THESE ALGORITHMS WE'VE DEVELOPED TO EVALUATE POTENTIAL THREATS--

--HAVE LED US *HERE.*

CLAY RAMSAY WAS FORCED TO ABSORB DANGEROUS AMOUNTS OF KRYPTONITE ENERGY. GAVE HIM SUPERPOWERS.

WHEN WE FOUGHT, HE CALLED HIMSELF *KRYPTONITE MAN.*

RAMSAY WAS IN AND OUT OF STRYKER'S FOR YEARS.

I SHOULD HAVE DONE MORE TO HELP HIM.

SUPERMAN, YOU KNOW AS WELL AS I DO...

...CLAY RAMSAY WAS A DEAD MAN WALKING THE MOMENT HE WAS CAUGHT IN THAT EXPLOSION.*

OVER THE YEARS, RAMSAY'S BODY WENT THROUGH SOME...*CHANGES.*** BUT LOOKS LIKE PORTIONS OF IT WERE INHUMED HERE.

BUT IF ANYONE WERE TO STEAL PORTIONS OF HIS BODY, THEY COULD SIPHON OFF ANY REMAINING KRYPTONITE RADIATION AND USE IT AS A WEAPON.

*WAY BACK IN ACTION COMICS ANNUAL #1.
**SEE SUPERWOMAN VOL. 1 FOR MORE...IT WAS GROSS. --PAUL

BUT...

...I CAN ALWAYS TELL WHEN I'M *NEAR* KRYPTONITE. AND RIGHT NOW, I'M FEELING...A HINT OF IT IN THE AIR.

THAT'S ODD. MY SCANNER SHOWS THE BODY IS CLEAN.

BUT WE ARE NOT THE ONLY PEOPLE TO CHECK THE GRAVE RECENTLY. SOMEONE WAS HERE...

...WITHIN THE LAST HOUR.

AND IT WOULD SEEM THEY'RE *STILL* HERE...

...BUT YOU DIDN'T EXPECT TO FIGHT *ME!*

KLANK

WHACK

ZZTT

HIS MASK HAS LEAD IN IT.

OF COURSE IT DOES. I RECOGNIZE THE FIGHTING STYLE.

VERY GOOD.

DETECTIVE.

GENERAL ZOD.

WHAT? ZOD...?

"ZOD IS OFF-PLANET. TRYING TO BUILD A NEW LIFE FAR FROM HERE."

I AM AWARE OF YOUR RECENT DEALINGS. MY GRANDSON IS FRIENDLY WITH *YOUR* BOY. AND I KEEP TABS ON WHO MY FAMILY CONSORTS WITH.

BUT I BELIEVE YOUR TRUCE WITH ZOD WAS...*HURRIED*, TO SAY THE LEAST.

IN FACT, THE GENERAL APPROACHED *ME* FOR AN ALLIANCE.

HE WANTED KANDOR.

IMPOSSIBLE.

"KANDOR WAS DESTROYED. ZOD KNOWS THIS...ALL THE LIVES LOST..."

A TRAGEDY, I'M SURE.

BUT THAT IS WHY *YOUR* ZOD WANTED *MY* HELP...

"HE DEMANDED TO USE MY LAZARUS PITS TO RESURRECT KANDOR.

"I HAVE NO NEED FOR A FALLEN GENERAL, AND IN FACT... I BELIEVE *MORE* KRYPTONIANS WOULD BE A WASTE OF OUR PLANET'S RESOURCES. SO I REJECTED HIS OFFER.

"I KNOW ALL TOO WELL WHAT THE LAZARUS PITS CAN DO TO A MAN. THE MADNESS THAT CORRUPTS EVEN THE GREATEST SOULS.

"ZOD FORCED MY HAND. I DESTROYED THE PIT HE WANTED. BUT THERE ARE MORE, AND HE WILL NOT REST UNTIL HE FINDS THEM.

AND IF YOU WILL NOT HELP ME TAKE CARE OF YOUR KIN, THEN I WILL FIND *OTHER* WAYS TO DEAL WITH THE KRYPTONIAN.

THERE IS *NO TIME* FOR OUR GAMES, DETECTIVE. ZOD IS ALREADY ON THE HUNT FOR A LAZARUS PIT AND I'M TRAILING BEHIND.

YOU'RE NOT GOING ANYWHERE EXCEPT TO THE *AUTHORITIES*, RA'S.

THEN *WE'LL* DEAL WITH ZOD.

THE BATPLANE IS ON THE WAY HERE--

DON'T BE SO HASTY, DETECTIVE. YOU DON'T KNOW THE LOCATIONS OF THE LAZARUS PITS--*I DO.*

FURTHERMORE, I HAVE DEDUCED WHICH HE'LL ATTEMPT TO STRIKE NEXT.

AND YOUR PLANE WON'T BE NECESSARY. YOU MUST KNOW...

"...YOU'RE NOT THE ONLY ONE WITH *TOYS*.

"WE'LL TAKE MY *DEMON WING*."

I KNOW YOU'RE LYING ABOUT SOMETHING, RA'S.

AND WHEN I FIND OUT WHAT, I WILL BREAK EVERY BONE IN YOUR DAMN BODY.

NEVER CHANGE, DETECTIVE.

BUT SEE FOR YOURSELF...

THE LOST TEMPLE OF QUETZALCÓATL!

TODAY I HOPE YOU TRUST I AM BEYOND DECEPTION-- OTHERWISE I WOULD NEVER *WILLINGLY* BRING YOU HERE.

MY X-RAY VISION CANNOT PIERCE ITS WALLS.

AND *THAT* IS WHY ZOD WILL LOOK *HERE*. YOUR ZOD IS A GENERAL OF WAR, TRAINED TO LOOK FOR WHAT IS OBVIOUSLY HIDDEN.

YOU USED *MAGIC* ON THE TEMPLE, DIDN'T YOU?

MY LAZARUS PITS ARE THE LIFE-BLOOD OF MY LEGACY. *NO ONE* CAN DISTURB THEM.

THEY'RE UNDER THE PROTECTION OF THE *LEAGUE OF LAZARUS.* MEN I HAVE PERSONALLY TRAINED SINCE BIRTH TO KEEP THE PITS SAFE.

IF ANYONE, HUMAN *OR* ALIEN, WERE TO BREACH THE OUTER DEFENSES, THESE ELITE SOLDIERS WOULD MAKE SHORT WORK OF THEM. THEY PROTECT THE PITS WITH THEIR--

...LIVES.

THERE'S STILL A PULSE.

BARELY.

MERCY FROM ZOD IS A GOOD SIGN.

AND YET, HE *DARES* EMBARRASS THE DEMON'S HEAD...

KRASH

THIS FIGHT ISN'T *DONE!*

AND WE WILL *NEVER* KNOW.

RA'S, YOU DON'T WANT TO GET IN THE MIDDLE OF TWO KRYPTONIANS.

ZOD-- WHY ARE YOU DOING THIS?

HOW CAN YOU QUESTION MY MOTIVES, KAL-EL?

OUR PEOPLE DESERVED BETTER THAN TO MEET AN UNCEREMONIOUS SLAUGHTER BY THAT MONGREL *ROGOL ZAAR.*

ZOD, I... I UNDERSTAND, BUT THIS ISN'T RIGHT. YOU CAN'T...

WAIT...

YOU SEE IT NOW, DON'T YOU?

THE CITY IS *ALREADY* EMPTY...

NO...

PLEASE TELL ME YOU HAVE KRYPTONITE ON YOU, DETECTIVE.

NOT ENOUGH FOR THIS...

YES...

BATMAN/SUPERMAN #8

cover by
NICK DERINGTON

I REMEMBER THAT DAY ON KRYPTON...

THE WINDS COMING IN FROM THE VALLEY WERE COLD AND LOUD...

...ONLY BROKEN BY MY FATHER'S VOICE...

YOUR MOTHER INFORMED ME THAT YOU DID WELL IN THIS SEASON'S WAR GAMES.

YOU BROUGHT HONOR TO THE HOUSE OF...

...ZOD.

IT WAS CLOSE. I NEARLY FAILED THE KANDORIAN CULTURE PORTION OF THAT EXAM...

WHY DO I NEED TO STUDY IT, FATHER?

KANDOR IS AN IMPORTANT PART OF THE HOUSE OF ZOD'S PAST.

SIT WITH ME.

ALLOW ME TO TELL YOU ABOUT KANDOR, MY SON...

PRESENT DAY.

THE LOST TEMPLE OF QUETZALCÓATL'S LAZARUS CHAMBER.

THE KANDOR COMPROMISE
PART TWO

SHUT UP AND PREPARE FOR BATTLE, YOU FOOL!

WHAT'RE YOU--

ZZPPPTT

KANDOR LIVES!

NO LONGER WILL YOUR LEGACY BE CAPTIVITY AND DEATH!

JOSHUA WILLIAMSON writer
NICK DERINGTON artist

DAVE McCAIG colorist **JOHN J. HILL** letterer
NICK DERINGTON cover
ANDY KUBERT & BRAD ANDERSON variant cover
BEN MEARES assistant editor **PAUL KAMINSKI** editor
BEN ABERNATHY group editor

SUPERMAN created by JERRY SIEGEL and JOE SHUSTER.
By special arrangement with the JERRY SIEGEL FAMILY.
BATMAN created by BOB KANE with BILL FINGER.

ZZPT-TSH

THEY HAVE POWERS ALREADY?!

COULD THE PITS HAVE TURNED THE DORMANT RED SUN ENERGY INTO YELLOW?

YOU HAD TO KNOW THIS WOULD HAPPEN, ZOD. HOW DID YOU PLAN TO CONTAIN THEM ONCE YOU--

KRASH

RAH!

SPLUT

WE CAN'T LET THEM LEAVE THE TEMPLE. *WHO KNOWS* WHAT WOULD HAPPEN TO THEM IF THEY WERE FREE IN THE WORLD!

THEN YOU KNOW THE *HARD TRUTH,* DETECTIVE.

THERE IS ONLY ONE SOLUTION TO THIS PROBLEM. WE USE KRYPTONITE TO *KILL* THE KANDORIANS...

"...BEFORE THEY KILL *US!*"

NO! ZOD!

WHY DID YOU DO THIS? WHY BRING BACK KANDOR LIKE THIS?

BECAUSE *YOU* DIDN'T...

...EVEN...

...TRY!

"AFTER ROGOL ZAAR MASSACRED OUR PEOPLE, YOU SCATTERED THEIR BODIES ACROSS THE COSMOS IN SOME WEAK TRIBUTE.

"BUT DURING MY IMPRISONMENT IN AMANDA WALLER'S SUICIDE SQUAD, I BECAME ACQUAINTED WITH A GREAT MANY OF YOUR ADOPTED WORLD'S SECRETS...

...INCLUDING THE *LAZARUS PITS!*

KANDOR DESERVED A SECOND CHANCE AT LIFE WITH A LEADER WHO WILL PROTECT THEM!

THE ONLY LIFE YOU'VE GIVEN THEM IS *MADNESS!*

EVEN WHEN THIS PASSES, THE LAZARUS PITS CORRUPT THE MIND AND SOUL! IT TAKES *YEARS* OF PAIN AND MISERY TO FULLY RECOVER!

THOOM

SUPERMAN, DESTROY THAT WALL!

I HAVE AN IDEA...

IT BETTER BE A *GOOD* IDEA, RA'S...

...BECAUSE I'M IN NO MOOD TO TAKE ORDERS FROM *YOU!*

YOU ALWAYS SEEM TO TAKE ORDERS FROM BATMAN. MY MISTAKE.

AH.

GOOD.

I BELIEVE I HAVE WHAT WE NEED IN MY ARMORY.

YOU WILL *NOT* HURT ANY OF--

IF YOU WISH FOR THEM TO REMAIN UNHARMED, YOU'LL WANT TO KEEP THEM FROM ESCAPING, SUPERMAN.

BOOM

WAIT! PLEASE! LISTEN TO ME, MY BROTHERS AND SISTERS.

I KNOW YOU'RE ANGRY. *SCARED.* BUT IF YOU LEAVE, YOU WILL BE IN *TERRIBLE DANGER.*

YOU CAN TRUST...

TNK

...ME...?

...NO...

SUPERMAN!

WHAT DID YOU DO, RA'S?

CALM YOURSELF, DETECTIVE.

I REALIZED I HAD AN ULTRAVIOLET-LIGHT GRENADE THAT REPLICATES THE EFFECTS OF A *RED SUN.*

IT WON'T LAST FOREVER, BUT LONG ENOUGH THAT I CAN STRIKE THEM DOWN AS THEY--

THUK

YOU SHOULD HAVE SIDED WITH ME FROM THE START, DEMON'S HEAD.

WE COULD HAVE MADE GREAT ALLIES.

IS KANDOR...?

LOOK ON, KAL-EL.

DESPITE YOUR FAILINGS...THE GLORY OF OUR GREAT KANDOR IS RESTORED.

POK

ZOD, LOOK *INSIDE* THE CITY...

"THE KANDORIANS ARE STILL *CRAZED*. WE HAVE NO IDEA WHAT THIS HAS DONE TO THEM. WHEN OR *IF* THEY WILL BE THEMSELVES AGAIN.

"THIS IS A DESECRATION OF WHAT YOU CLAIM TO LOVE ABOUT KANDOR.

HOW COULD YOU DO THIS?

HAVEN'T THEY BEEN THROUGH ENOUGH ALREADY?

REMOVE YOUR FINGER FROM MY CHEST, KAL-EL.

YOU CLAIM THIS WAS FOR KANDOR. THAT YOU WERE WILLING TO TAKE THE ABUSE TO SAVE OUR PEOPLE.

BUT YOU DIDN'T DO THIS FOR *THEM*.

THIS IS ABOUT *YOU*. AN *ARROGANT*, SELFISH ACT... FOR WHAT?

YOU YOURSELF HAVE RISEN FROM THE GRAVE, KAL-EL.

AND YOU, BATMAN. I KNOW THAT YOU HAVE HAD LOVED ONES RETURNED TO YOU BECAUSE OF THE PITS.

WOULD EITHER OF YOU REJECT THOSE GIFTS? KNOWING WHAT YOU *KNOW?*

SLICE

STRASH

WHAT HAVE YOU DONE?!

DEATH IS *MINE* TO DENY.

NO ONE ELSE'S.

ZOD...

KRASH

BATMAN, I NEED TO GET KANDOR TO THE FORTRESS RIGHT NOW IF WE WANT ANY HOPE OF--

GO.

I'LL DEAL WITH THE GENERAL AND THE DEMON!

WHOOSH

YOUR NAME MEANS "THE *DEMON'S HEAD*," YES? I WONDER...

...WHAT THEY'LL CALL YOU ONCE YOU'RE **HEADLESS!**

THAP

POOM

ARROGANT HUMAN! YOU THINK YOU STAND A *CHANCE* AGAINST A KRYPTONIAN?!

SUPERMAN AND I MAY HAVE SPARRED ONCE OR TWICE. I HELD MY OWN.

AND KAL-EL LET YOU LIVE? HOW DID YOU STAND A CHANCE?

DID YOU FORGET SO EASILY, ALIEN?

KRYPTONITE!

SLASH

HM.

IT'S BEEN A LONG TIME SINCE I'VE BEEN HURT LIKE THIS.

KNEEL BEFORE RA'S AL GHUL!

BUT I'M NOT *THAT* HURT.

URK!

EVEN YOUR LAZARUS PITS CAN'T SAVE YOU FROM WHAT I'M ABOUT TO DO, HUMAN.

ZOD, *WAIT!*

I KNOW WHAT YOU'RE FEELING.

HOW LOSS CAN DRIVE SOMEONE TO EXTREMES.

IT CAN TURN INTO AN INCREDIBLE ANGER THAT CONSUMES YOU! I'M SURE THAT IS WHAT YOU FELT WHEN KRYPTON WAS DESTROYED. AND NOW WITH KANDOR.

BUT THIS IS *NOT* JUSTICE FOR KANDOR.

SUPERMAN TOLD ME HOW YOU HAVE WORKED TO BE A BETTER MAN.

KILLING RA'S WON'T BRING BACK WHAT YOU HAVE LOST. IT WILL NOT BRING YOU PEACE *OR* CHANGE KANDOR'S PAST...

TELL KAL-EL THAT I WILL HONOR OUR TRUCE.

BUT TO STAY AWAY FROM JEKUUL.

"IT HAD TO BE YOU, BATMAN. AS MUCH AS I WISH I COULD, I CAN NEVER RELATE TO ZOD'S ANGER. NOT THE WAY YOU CAN."

"WHAT HAPPENED TO RA'S AL GHUL?"

"MY WORRY WAS THAT HE WAS INJURED AND WOULD FLEE TO THE LAZARUS PITS.

"BUT HE IS EVER RESOURCEFUL.

"EVEN FROM THAT DISTANCE I COULD TELL HE WAS EMBARRASSED."

"EMBARRASSED?"

"I SAVED HIM FROM ZOD."

WHILE *I* SAVED KANDOR.

AS MUCH AS I COULD, AT LEAST.

THERE'S NO TELLING WHAT THE LAZARUS PITS DID TO THEM. IF THEY WOULD REMEMBER WHO THEY WERE. HURT THEMSELVES... OR OTHERS.

SO DID YOU...?

"THE FORTRESS WAS ABLE TO PUT THEM INTO A STASIS TO PROTECT THEM. NOT ALIVE AND NOT DEAD. A KIND OF COSMIC COMA UNTIL WE CAN HELP THEM.

BUT THERE'S *MORE.*

THIS MINIATURE CITY... IT'S A *REPRO-DUCTION...*

...AND HALF OF THE KANDORIAN POPULATION IS *MISSING.*

"ZOD DID NOT PUT *ALL* THE KANDORIANS INTO THE LAZARUS PITS TODAY.

"HE KNEW KANDOR WOULD BE DRIVEN TO MADNESS AND TOOK A CALCULATED RISK.

"I'M POSITIVE THAT IS THE REASON HE LEFT WITHOUT A FIGHT. HE HAD THE REST OF THE KANDORIAN BODIES HIDDEN AWAY...

"...WITH ENOUGH SAMPLES OF THE LAZAPUS PIT MATERIAL TO ATTEMPT ANOTHER REVIVAL.

"THEY'LL NEED TO BE PLACED IN THE SAME TYPE OF STASIS AS OUR HALF IF THEY EVER WANT TO HAVE ANY HOPE OF A *TRUE* REVIVAL."

I CAN HAVE LUCIUS PREP THE BATROCKET. ZOD IS *NOT* PLAYING US. NOT TODAY.

I *KNEW*, BATMAN.

YOU KNEW?

I *GUESSED*. THERE WAS NO WAY HE WAS LEAVING EARTH EMPTY-HANDED...BUT IF THIS TRUCE IS REAL, THEN THERE'S MUTUAL TRUST I MUST RESPECT.

YOU MEAN *MUTUALLY ASSURED DESTRUCTION.*

IT'S NOT *THAT*, BATMAN. IT'S A COMPROMISE.

"THE *KANDOR* COMPROMISE..."

IS THIS HOW WE HONOR THE DEAD NOW? *COMPROMISE?*

IT HELPS US HONOR THE LIVING, BATMAN.

ZOD IS A MAN OF WAR, BUT NOT VIOLENCE. HE FIGHTS FOR WHAT HE BELIEVES IN, AND I HOPE...

BATMAN/SUPERMAN #9

cover by
CLAYTON HENRY and **ALEJANDRO SÁNCHEZ**

NOT ANOTHER ONE.

MY GOD...

LOOK AT HIM... THE WIRES AND...

JUST DON'T *TOUCH* HIM, OKAY?

GOTHAM HARBOR.

MIGHT AS WELL TELL BULLOCK TO LIGHT THE SIGNAL NOW.

DAMN. YEAH.

WHAT KIND OF MONSTER DOES THIS TO ANOTHER HUMAN BEING?

THIS IS GOTHAM, BUDDY...

BECAUSE IF YOU CAN SURVIVE IN GOTHAM...

...YOU CAN SURVIVE ANYWHERE.

VVRRROMMM-MM

SKULL! STOP RIGHT--

NO! THERE'S NO TIME--I'M TRYING TO HELP!

ATOMIC SKULL WAS ONCE ALBERT MICHAELS.

A RADIOACTIVE BLAST TURNED HIM INTO THIS. HE FOUGHT SUPERMAN. BUT AFTER SOME JAIL TIME HE HAD SUPPOSEDLY REFORMED. EVEN JOINED THE METROPOLIS P.D. WISH I COULD SAY I'M SURPRISED IT DIDN'T STICK.

LAST KNOWN SIGHTING WAS MONTHS AGO.

I DON'T WANT TO FIGHT ANYONE, BATMAN.

BUT I CAN'T LET THEM TAKE ME BACK!

THOUGHT YOU TURNED OVER A NEW LEAF, SKULL?

YOU DON'T UNDER-STAND!

I WAS LIVING A HAPPY LIFE. AWAY FROM ALL THE FIGHTS AND DEATH...

...BUT HE WOULDN'T LET ME!

FWWOSHH

I'M NOT... I'M *NOT* A BAD GUY.

I DIDN'T EVEN KILL THOSE PSYCHO KIDS, AND I TOTALLY COULD HAVE...*

BUT IT'S HARD TO THINK STRAIGHT NOW.

HE--HE DID SOMETHING TO ME. TO MY *MIND.*

*SKULL IS REFERRING TO HIS TIME AS A CAPTIVE OF THE TEEN TITANS! -- PAUL

BATMAN?

WH-- WHERE DID YOU GO?

...THAT THEY SMELL LIKE *DEATH*.

THESE LOOK LIKE REMOTE-CONTROLLED DRONES.

I NEED TO GET THEM BACK TO THE CAVE TO STUDY.

NO! THERE'S MORE TO IT, BATMAN. YOU NEED TO *RUN.*

I ESCAPED SO I COULD WARN YOU. THEY ARE COMING FOR *YOU* NEXT. HE'S FURIOUS AND HE'S GOING TO HURT SUPERMAN, USING *YOU.*

WHO IS?

PLEASE TELL MAGGIE I SAID THANK YOU AND THAT I'M SORR--

SORRY, LOIS. WE CAN--

OH NO, I KNOW THAT FACE.

GOTHAM.

GO.

WHOOSH

SORRY, BOYS. SHOW'S OVER.

GOTHAM IS UNDER BATMAN'S WATCH, SO I DON'T NORMALLY KEEP AN EAR ON IT...

GOTHAM HARBOR.

BATMAN/SUPERMAN #10

cover by
CLAYTON HENRY and **ALEJANDRO SÁNCHEZ**

ONCE UPON A TIME IN METROPOLIS.

AND I HAD FAITH IN ALBERT MICHAELS.

THE BATCAVE. TODAY.

YEARS AGO, HE WAS HIT BY AN ATOMIC BLAST. IT TRANSFORMED HIS BODY INTO SOMETHING HORRIFIC--THE *ATOMIC SKULL.* AT FIRST HE LIVED THE LIFE OF A *VILLAIN*...BUT HE WORKED TO BETTER HIMSELF. HE SHOWED ME THAT HE WANTED TO BE A *HERO.*

LAST NIGHT HE EXPLODED... TAKING A CHUNK OF GOTHAM WITH HIM. NEARLY KILLING BATMAN. HUNDREDS COULD HAVE DIED, IF I HADN'T ARRIVED IN TIME.

BRUCE HASN'T SAID A WORD SINCE WE GOT ATOMIC SKULL'S BODY TO THE BATCAVE. I CAN'T TELL IF HE'S IGNORING ME OR LOST IN THOUGHT AS HE SCANS.

BUT IT'S NOT LIKE WE'VE TALKED MUCH THE LAST FEW WEEKS ANYWAY...

ATOMIC PART TWO

JOSHUA WILLIAMSON writer **CLAYTON HENRY** artist **ALEJANDRO SANCHEZ** colorist
JOHN J. HILL letterer **HENRY & SANCHEZ** cover **RICCARDO FEDERICI** variant cover
BEN MEARES assistant editor **PAUL KAMINSKI** editor **BEN ABERNATHY** group editor
SUPERMAN created by JERRY SIEGEL and JOE SHUSTER. By special arrangement with the Jerry Siegel Family.
BATMAN created by BOB KANE with BILL FINGER

GOTHAM
INDUSTRIAL
CLEAN WASTE.

IT'S THE LARGEST DISPOSAL
OF INDUSTRIAL DISCARD IN
THE UNITED STATES. ITEMS
THAT CAN'T BE PROCESSED
AND DISPOSED OF AT ANY
KIND OF LOCAL LEVEL ARE
SENT HERE TO BE RECYCLED.

I'VE USED IT TO DISPOSE OF
QUITE A FEW DANGEROUS ELEMENTS. FOR
EXAMPLE, THE JOKER'S LAUGHING GAS.
A LOT OF THE DAMAGE FROM BANE'S
TAKEOVER OF THE CITY WAS SENT HERE.

AND IT'S WHERE ALL THE COMPANIES
WHO MADE THOSE PARTS SEND OUTDATED
TECHNOLOGY. IT IS ONE OF THE MOST
SECURE LOCATIONS IN GOTHAM.

...THE ULTRA-HUMANITE.

"I COULD NEVER UNCOVER HIS REAL NAME, BUT I KNOW HE WAS A SCIENTIST. CONFINED TO A WHEELCHAIR, HE EXPERIMENTED ON HIMSELF. HE COULD HAVE USED HIS GENIUS FOR GOOD, BUT HE HAD OTHER, MORE *SINISTER* INTENTIONS.

"HE STARTED OFF BY TURNING AN ORGANIZED CRIME RING INTO AN EVIL EMPIRE FOCUSED ON WORLD DOMINATION. BUT THAT WASN'T GOOD ENOUGH. HE WANTED *MORE*

"IT WAS CLEAR TO ME THAT HIS STRUGGLES MADE HIM ANGRY WITH THE WORLD, SO HE WANTED TO *CONTROL* WHATEVER HE COULD. USED HIS GENIUS TO CREATE A NEW BODY FOR HIMSELF. ONE THAT LET HIM FEEL *STRONG*.

"I FOUGHT HIM A FEW TIMES OVER THE YEARS.

"LAST I SAW HE WAS WITH THE *SECRET SOCIETY*."

WHY WOULD THE *ULTRA-HUMANITE* BE IN GOTHAM?

IT WARMS MY HEART TO HEAR YOU SPEAK MY NAME...

AND I WILL

SHOW YOU

WHAT A *TRUE* GENIUS

IS CAPABLE OF!

THE DECOMPOSITION SHOWS THEY WERE DEAD *BEFORE* THEY WERE ALTERED.

WHO KNOWS WHEN HE TOOK OVER THE PLANT!

KRAK

FLOOSH

AND I HAVE NO PROBLEM BLOWING UP GOTHAM TO DO IT!

SUPERMAN, YOU NEED TO GET THAT DRONE OUT OF THE CITY.

NOW.

ON IT!

"...BUT I RARELY HAVE ANYONE TO SPEAK TO.

YOU MUST UNDERSTAND *WHY* I DO WHAT I DO.

IT HAS BEEN MY LIFE'S WORK TO PROVE THAT MY MIND WAS GREATER THAN THE BODY I WAS TRAPPED IN.

I KNOW, I KNOW... "PROVE TO WHOM," YOU MIGHT ASK.

TO *MYSELF,* TO BE HONEST.

WHAT...?

BUT EVERY ATTEMPT HAS LED TO FAILURE.

WHAT THE--?

THINK AGAIN.

SHR?P

=SIGH= MUST WE GO THROUGH THE MOTIONS HERE, REALLY? THIS WILL ALL BE MUCH EASIER IF YOU JUST DO WHAT I TELL YOU TO DO.

I'M NOT GOING TO LET YOU TURN ME INTO SOME BOMB LIKE YOU DID TO ATOMIC SKULL AND THOSE SICK DRONES, ULTRA-HUMANITE.

OH, HOW I DO ENJOY BEING A PROPER VILLAIN.

BEEP

BATMAN/SUPERMAN #11

cover by
DAVID MARQUEZ

GOTHAM FINANCIAL DISTRICT.
EPICENTER OF THE ATOMIC SKULL EXPLOSION.

THIS FEELS LIKE A BAD IDEA, MAN.

RELAX. THE COPS GOT BIGGER THINGS TO WORRY ABOUT THAN THIS BANK. THEY'RE TOO CONCERNED WITH CHECKING FOR SURVIVORS IN THE WRECKAGE.

YEAH, BUT TAKING ADVANTAGE OF THE EXPLOSION...

MAYBE WE'LL DONATE SOME OF THIS TO CHARITY. WILL *THAT* MAKE YOU FEEL BETTER?

NOW C'MON...NO-BODY IS OUT HERE. WE'RE FREE AND--

WHAT THE--?!

RUN.

GET OUT OF HERE WHILE YOU STILL CAN!

"CAN YOU FEEL IT, BATMAN?"

"THE STRENGTH THAT FLOWS THROUGH YOUR VEINS?"

ATOMIC CONCLUSION

JOSHUA WILLIAMSON writer   CLAYTON HENRY artist
ALEJANDRO SANCHEZ colorist   JOHN J. HILL letterer
DAVID MARQUEZ cover   JAE LEE & JUNE CHUNG variant cover
BEN MEARES assistant editor   PAUL KAMINSKI editor
BEN ABERNATHY group editor

SUPERMAN created by JERRY SIEGEL and JOE SHUSTER.
By special arrangement with the Jerry Siegel Family.
BATMAN created by BOB KANE with BILL FINGER.

...BOOM.

FLOOSH

AH!!

BATMAN, JUST HANG ON! I'LL--

NO!

YOU SAW THAT DETONATOR *INSIDE* ATOMIC SKULL'S REMAINS. IT TURNED HIM INTO A BOMB THAT TOOK OUT PART OF GOTHAM. YOU NEED TO GET ME OUT OF THE CITY BEFORE IT'S TOO LATE.

THE CLOCK IS TICKING, SUPERMAN.

YOUR FRIEND IS ABOUT TO BLOW UP. YOU *KNOW* WHAT YOU NEED TO DO.

HE'S RIGHT.

YOU *KNOW* HE'S RIGHT!

I...I CAN'T. I *WON'T!*

BATMAN...I'M SORRY ABOUT BEFORE. YOU WERE *RIGHT.*

I SHOULD HAVE TALKED TO YOU ABOUT REVEALING TO THE WORLD THAT I WAS CLARK KENT. I SHOULD HAVE--

DO IT!

HAHA HAHA! PERFECTION!

I KNEW MY PLANS WOULD LEAD TO YOUR EMBARRASSMENT, BUT NEVER IN MY WILDEST DREAMS DID I THINK YOU WOULD ACTUALLY *KILL BATMAN!*

WHEN I WAS IN HIS MIND, I COULD FEEL WHAT HE THOUGHT OF YOU. THE RESPECT AND ADMIRATION HE CARRIED FOR YOU.

I KNEW YOU WORKED TOGETHER, BUT IT NEVER OCCURRED TO ME THAT YOU WERE *FRIENDS.*

AND NOW HIS DEATH IS PART OF *MY* LEGACY.

THIS IS MY LEGACY.

MY VICTORY.

"A MYSTERIOUS JAILER HAD IMPRISONED ATOMIC SKULL. LOCKED HIM AWAY AGAINST HIS WILL. YOU MIGHT HAVE SEEN A MAN TRYING TO REDEEM HIMSELF, BUT *THEY* ONLY SAW THE MONSTER. THEY TRIED TO CHANGE HIM. TAKE AWAY *WHO* HE WAS.*

*AS SEEN IN THE PAGES OF TEEN TITANS. --PAUL

"HE HAD BEEN BANISHED TO THE TUNDRA, HIS OLD LIFE ERASED FROM HIS MIND. THEY COULD HIDE WHO HE WAS ON THE OUTSIDE, BUT IN THE END THEY COULDN'T HIDE THE RADIATION *INSIDE* OF HIM.

"RADIATION *I* NEEDED."

WHO... *WHO ARE YOU?*

SOME- ONE WHO CAN HELP YOU. HELP YOU REDISCOVER WHO YOU *REALLY ARE.*

"AND I DID. I UNLOCKED HIS MIND.

"AND WITHIN I DISCOVERED THAT NOT ONLY COULD I HARNESS THAT RADIATION, BUT I COULD USE IT TO *KILL YOU,* SUPERMAN.

"ONCE ATOMIC SKULL LEARNED OF MY PLANS, HE FLED. ESCAPED INTO GOTHAM IN HOPES OF WARNING YOU.

"I HAD NO CHOICE BUT TO *DETONATE* HIM."

IS IT?!

TZZZZ

BATMAN? HOW? YOU...

YOU SAW WHAT YOU *WANTED* TO SEE, ULTRA-HUMANITE. BUT YOU DIDN'T *HEAR* WHAT I HEARD.

BATMAN REMINDED ME OF THE DETONATOR WE FOUND INSIDE OF ATOMIC SKULL.

I USED MY X-RAY AND MICRO-SCOPIC VISION TO PINPOINT THE DETONATOR AND THEN USED A *VERY* THIN BLAST OF HEAT VISION DIRECTLY INTO BATMAN'S CHEST TO DESTROY IT.

"IT WAS A RISK, BUT WORTH IT.

GOOD TO SEE YOU, SUPERMAN.

HOW'D IT GO?

AS WELL AS COULD BE EXPECTED, LUCIUS.

"I RETURNED THE BODIES THAT ULTRA-HUMANITE STOLE. MOST OF THEM WERE FROM GRAVEYARDS IN GOTHAM. IT WAS HARD FOR PEOPLE TO KNOW THEIR LOVED ONES WERE ROBBED OF THEIR FINAL RESTING PLACE...BUT AT LEAST THEY WERE HOME *NOW*.

"*S.T.A.R. LABS* HAS ULTRA-HUMANITE'S BRAIN UNDER OBSERVATION. IT'S CONNECTED TO A NETWORK UNLIKE ANYTHING THEY'VE EVER SEEN. THERE COULD BE WHO KNOWS HOW MANY DRONES STILL OUT THERE.

"FRANKLY, THE BRAIN MATTER SHOULD BE DEAD. BUT SOMETHING ABOUT ATOMIC SKULL'S RADIATION SIGNATURE IS DISPLAYING REGENERATIVE PROPERTIES. IT'S BAFFLING EVERYONE.

"ATOMIC SKULL'S BODY IS SAFE AT STRYKER'S ISLAND'S GRAVEYARD. BY ESCAPING ULTRA-HUMANITE, HE SAVED LIVES. IT WAS IMPORTANT TO ME THAT THE WORLD UNDERSTAND WHO HE REALLY WAS.

"ATOMIC SKULL DIED A HERO. I HOPE HE KNOWS THAT.

LUCIUS... SHOULDN'T SOMEONE BE *HELPING HIM* WITH THE SURGERY?

YOU EVER TRY TELLING HIM HE CAN'T DO SOMETHING HIMSELF?

RELAX, YOU TWO...

AND WE WILL.

BUT RIGHT NOW, YOU'RE PINNED DOWN AND HAVE TO LISTEN TO ME FOR A MINUTE.

"WE'VE BOTH BEEN THROUGH A LOT OF HEARTACHE RECENTLY.

"A LOT OF CHANGES.

"AND SOMETIMES WHEN THAT HAPPENS, WE GET BUSY AND THEN WE GO OFF INTO OUR OWN LITTLE CORNERS OF THE WORLD AND DON'T TALK TO EACH OTHER.

WE DON'T HAVE TO *ONLY* TALK ABOUT OUR CASES...

CLARK, STOP. I KNOW THAT. AND I WASN'T MAD THAT YOU DIDN'T CONSULT WITH ME ABOUT REVEALING YOUR IDENTITY. I WAS ONLY FRUSTRATED WITH HOW I REACTED.

ALBERT MICHAELS
THE ATOMIC SKULL

HE DIED A HERO.

"NO MATTER WHAT CHANGES HAPPEN IN OUR LIVES OR WHAT INSANE CASES TRY TO TEST US..."

BATMAN/SUPERMAN #12

cover by
DAVID MARQUEZ

WELL?

STEEL RECOGNIZED.

BATWOMAN RECOGNIZED.

ACCESS GRANTED.

WHOSE VOICE IS THAT?

A FRIEND WHO RECENTLY PASSED.

DARK.

CAN YOU READ ME? THIS BETTER WORK...

REVVV

HM.

THE SYSTEMS IN THE BATCAVE ARE--

VVVRRRRR

BATMAN...?

NOT ME.

KRUNCH

IS THE RESPONSOMETER CAUSING THIS?

LET'S FIND OUT!

KRTSH

THAT SHOULD--

HOLD ON...DO YOU HEAR THAT?

YOUR ARMORED SUIT IS EMPTY!

THEN WHAT ARE YOU WAITING FOR?!

ZZZZTTTT

SORRY TO DESTROY ANOTHER ONE OF YOUR TOYS!

KZZZTIZZZ

THHOOSSSH

I CAN BUILD ANOTHER ONE--AGH!

KZZZKZZ

REQUEST DENIED.

OOSSSSHHHH

SON--

--OF A--

YOUR BATCAVE TRIED TO KILL US.

SOMEONE OR SOME*THING* HACKED THE BAT-COMPUTER.

IS THAT POSSIBLE?

MAYBE *TWO* PEOPLE IN THE WHOLE WORLD ARE CAPABLE, AND I'D RECOGNIZE TIM'S OR BARBARA'S--

--WAIT. THE THREAT DATABASE... IT'S BEEN COMPROMISED. *STOLEN.*

IT'S A *VIRUS* UNLIKE ANY I'VE EVER SEEN.

I DON'T KNOW HOW IT FOUND ITS WAY INTO MY SYSTEMS BUT...

IT'S FROM *KANDOR.*

IT'S SAYING ONE WORD OVER AND OVER AGAIN.

...IT'S KRYPTONIAN.

I'M FLUENT IN YOUR NATIVE LANGUAGE, BUT I DON'T RECOGNIZE THE PHRASING HERE.

BRAINIAC.

I THOUGHT BRAINIAC WAS LUTHOR'S RIGHT-HAND MAN NOWADAYS.*

SUPERGIRL HAD SOME PROBLEMS WITH HIM AS WELL.**

AND NOW HE DID *ALL THIS*?

WHY DIDN'T THEY TELL THE JUSTICE LEAGUE? TELL *ANYONE*?

AND WHY WERE *WE* THE ONLY ONES TO GET THE SIGNAL TO COME TO THE CAVE?

*SEE JUSTICE LEAGUE: THE JUSTICE/DOOM WAR.

**AS SEEN IN SUPERGIRL VOL.3: INFECTIOUS.

WHEN THE BOTTLED CITY OF KANDOR WAS RESTORED, IT SENT OUT AN AGES-OLD BRAINIAC SIGNAL THAT INFILTRATED THE JUSTICE LEAGUE NETWORK AND ACCESSED THE BATCAVE.

I DON'T KNOW WHAT IT WAS SEARCHING FOR, BUT IT MERGED WITH THE VILLAIN DATABASE WE BUILT, CREATING SOME KIND OF COMPOSITE VIRUS THAT *ATTACKED* US.

BUT IT LEFT A TRAIL.

SUPERMAN AND I ⇒KRT⇐ TO THE MOON. ⇒KZZTT⇐ WHAT WE FOUND ⇒KKZZZT⇐ IMPRESSIVE *BUT* DANGEROUS...

I RECORDED THIS MESSAGE IN CASE WE DID NOT RETURN WITHIN 24 HOURS. IF YOU CAN HEAR THIS, WE NEED YOU TO--

KRTSH

--TO THE DARK SIDE OF THE MOON AND--

DAMN. THEY FOUND ME. I HAVE TO STAY ON THE MOVE BEFORE THEY--

KZZT

WE GOTTA FOLLOW THAT SIGNAL AND WE GOTTA DO IT NOW.

NOT A FAN OF BEING DRAFTED OR FOLLOWING ORDERS BLINDLY.

BUT IF BATMAN AND SUPERMAN ARE IN DANGER, THEN IT LOOKS LIKE A JOB FOR...

"HEY, NAT, IT'S UNCLE JOHN. I GOT A FAVOR TO ASK.

"ARE YOU FINISHED BUILDING THAT NEW SPACESHIP FOR THE TITANS AND THE LEAGUE?"

"YOU COOL IF I TAKE IT FOR A TEST DRIVE?"

PLANET BRAINIAC

PART ONE

JOSHUA WILLIAMSON
writer

MAX RAYNOR
artist

ALEJANDRO SANCHEZ
colorist

JOHN J. HILL
letterer

DAVID MARQUEZ
cover

LEE WEEKS &
ELIZABETH BREITWEISER
variant cover

BEN MEARES
assistant editor

PAUL KAMINSKI
editor

BEN ABERNATHY
group editor

...TO *NOT* FOLLOW US TO THE MOON.

BATMAN/SUPERMAN #13

cover by
DAVID MARQUEZ and **ALEJANDRO SÁNCHEZ**

FIRST TIME IN SPACE?

I PREFER TO SEE THE STARS FROM ROOFTOPS.

YOU?

SPACE? OH YEAH, MORE TIMES THAN I CAN COUNT.

BUT NO MATTER HOW MANY TIMES, IT'S STILL SPECIAL.

ALMOST MAKES ALL THE CRAZINESS WORTH IT...

HM. THE JUSTICE LEAGUE SPACECRAFT IS PICKING UP SOME READINGS AHEAD.

THAT MUST BE WHERE BATMAN AND SUPERMAN TRACKED BRAINIAC'S PROGRAM.

BUT HOW DID THE BRAINIAC PROGRAM TAKE THEM DOWN?

DOOMSDAY?!

THAT'S NEW!

KKRRISSSHH

UGH.

KRASH.

BATWOMAN?!

CRAP, LOST MY HAMMER IN THE--

RRRGGGHHH!

...CHECKMATE.

TEST COMPLETED.

RESTRAINTS DISENGAGED.

HOW DID YOU KNOW?

YOU WERE ATTEMPTING TO USE THE RIDDLES TO DISTRACT ME FROM THE GAME.

HOWEVER, THE RIDDLES WERE CLUES TO YOUR NEXT MOVES.

LEADING ME TO CHECKMATE.

LIKE THE *REAL* RIDDLER, YOUR COMPULSION GAVE YOU AWAY.

VERY GOOD.

NEXT TEST.

BEEP BEEP BEEP BEEP

BEEP BEEP

YOU WON'T BE NEEDING *THIS* ANYMORE, "RIDDLER."

BOOM

YOU CREATED THE PROGRAM I MERGED WITH TO BETTER UNDERSTAND YOUR ENEMIES. TO PREDICT THEIR MOVES. AND I MUST FULFILL THAT FUNCTION.

BUT IT IS CLEAR YOUR BATTLES ARE NEVER-ENDING. I MUST ACT AND LEARN QUICKLY IF I AM TO TRULY HELP YOU PUT AN END TO YOUR ENEMIES.

YOU HAVE PASSED MANY OF MY TESTS.

NOW I HAVE QUESTIONS.

YOU CLOAK YOURSELF IN SHADOWS AND YET YOU CALL YOURSELF A HERO.

YOU BREAK THE LAW...YOU REBEL AGAINST NORMALCY.

WHY?

I HAVE A CODE. I WANT TO SAVE LIVES. MAKE SURE WHAT HAPPENED TO ME NEVER HAPPENS TO ANYONE ELSE.

TRAUMA DRIVES YOU?

BUT TRAUMA ALSO INFORMS THE ACTIONS OF YOUR ENEMIES.

WHY DID YOU CHOOSE A DIFFERENT PATH?

WE'RE DONE HERE.

YOU REALLY WANT TO KNOW WHAT A *TRUE* VILLAIN IS?

LET'S JUST CUT TO THE CHASE.

ACCESS FILE: JOKER.

IF YOU INSIST.

HA.

HA ≥KZT≤ HA!

HA HA HA HA HA HA!

OKAY, I MIGHT ENJOY BEATING THIS ONE UP.

WHAT IS--?

I TRICKED THE PROGRAM INTO CREATING A *JOKER.* THE JOKER IS A CHAOS ENGINE THAT EVEN THE SMARTEST COMPUTER WILL NEVER UNDERSTAND.

ONCE I GOT MY HANDS ON IT, I DID SOME LIGHT REPROGRAMMING TO CAUSE CHALLENGES IN BRAINIAC'S PROGRAM.

YOU MADE A *VIRUS.*

I JUST WOUND HIM UP AND LET HIM GO. BUYS US SOME TIME.

NEVER THOUGHT I'D SAY THIS, BUT... I'LL LET THE JOKER PLAY FOR A BIT.

BATMAN. YOU HAVE COMPROMISED MY SYSTEMS AND THE TESTING.

WE WILL NOW HAVE TO START OVER.

WE'RE DONE WITH YOUR *TEST.*

THEN YOU FORCE MY HAND.

IF YOU WON'T COMPLY, I MUST--

STEEL? BATWOMAN?

DAMMIT.

HOW DID YOU FIND US IN THIS LABYRINTH?

ONCE WHEN I WAS A KID, I GOT LOST IN A HEDGE MAZE.

I LEARNED TO PULL THE TREES OUT OF THE GROUND AND MAKE MY OWN PATH.

GOOD TO SEE YOU, JOHN HENRY.

WHAT ARE YOU DOING HERE?

YOU'RE WELCOME.

MY ORDERS WERE FOR *NO ONE* TO COME HERE.

WE GOT YOUR DISTRESS BEACON TELLING US TO COME AND RESCUE YOU.

I INTERFERED WITH THE SIGNAL.

IT WAS MY HOPE TO FINISH THE PROGRAMMING YOU CREATED, BATMAN.

TO HELP YOU PREDICT THREATS.

TO DO THAT, I NEEDED MORE EXAMPLES OF HEROES TO COMPARE. TO STUDY. ALLOWING BATWOMAN AND STEEL TO COME HERE ASSISTED WITH THAT.

PLANET
BRAINIAC
PART TWO

...I MUST BECOME ONE.

JOSHUA WILLIAMSON
writer

MAX RAYNOR
artist

ALEJANDRO SANCHEZ
colorist

JOHN J. HILL
letterer

DAVID MARQUEZ and
ALEJANDRO SANCHEZ
cover

MARK BROOKS
variant cover

BEN MEARES
assistant editor

PAUL KAMINSKI
editor

BEN ABERNATHY
group editor

BATMAN/SUPERMAN #14

cover by
DAVID MARQUEZ and **ALEJANDRO SÁNCHEZ**

THEN...

ACTIVATE?
Y/N?

YOU ->KRTSH<- SURE ->KRK<- IS A GOOD IDEA ->KRTSH<- BATMAN?

BEEP

CREATING A DATABASE TO PROFILE AND PREDICT THREATS SEEMS LIKE SOMETHING WE NEED, AT *FIRST GLANCE*...

...BUT YOU TRIED PROGRAMS LIKE THIS BEFORE AND IT CAME BACK TO BITE YOU *HARD*.

WHY WILL THIS TIME BE ANY DIFFERENT?

AFTER EVERYTHING THAT HAPPENED WITH *THE BATMAN WHO LAUGHS**, WE OWE IT TO OURSELVES...TO THE *WORLD*...TO TRY AGAIN.

TO FIND *NEW* WAYS TO STOP OUR ENEMIES FROM HURTING INNOCENT PEOPLE, SUPERMAN.

*SEE BATMAN/SUPERMAN VOL. 1: WHO ARE THE SECRET SIX? --PAUL

AS FOR HOW THIS TIME WILL BE DIFFERENT...I HAVE AN IDEA.

YOU ALWAYS DO.

IF THIS PROGRAM FULFILLS ITS MISSION, WE CAN *PROUDLY* SAY...

"...IT HELPED MAKE THE WORLD A BETTER PLACE."

NOW. THE MOON.

DON'T HOLD BACK--THESE ROBOTS AREN'T REAL PEOPLE. WE NEED TO PUT THEM DOWN HARD!

STILL FEELS REAL WHEN THEY HIT US, BATWOMAN!

PLANET BRAINIAC
PART THREE

JOSHUA WILLIAMSON
writer

MAX RAYNOR
artist

ALEJANDRO SÁNCHEZ
colorist

JOHN J. HILL
letterer

DAVID MARQUEZ &
ALEJANDRO SÁNCHEZ
cover

BRYAN HITCH &
ALEX SINCLAIR
variant cover

BEN MEARES
assistant editor

PAUL KAMINSKI
editor

BEN ABERNATHY
group editor

ZZZZZZZ **BOOM**

NICE WORK, STEEL. E.M.P. WAVE?

YES, MA'AM

IT'S A *HUGE* DRAIN ON MY SUIT'S POWER AND I CAN ONLY USE IT ONCE.

HURTS LIKE *HELL* BUT SHOULD BUY US A FEW MINUTES.

IT'S APPRECIATED, STEEL.

BATWOMAN WAS RIGHT. THE PROGRAM IS ACTING LIKE A CHILD. WHICH MEANS I DON'T NEED TO *FIGHT* IT.

I NEED TO *TALK* TO IT.

JOHN HENRY. CAN YOU HELP ME *HACK* AN ARMY OF KILLER ROBOTS?

I THOUGHT YOU'D NEVER ASK.

HOPEFULLY SUPERMAN HAS YOUR COMPOSITE UNDER CONTROL.

WHY ARE YOU WEARING THEIR COSTUMES?!

BECAUSE THEY MADE ME.

THEY'D NEVER DO THAT. SUPERMAN IS GOING TO *GET* YOU.

GOOD.

I WOULD HARDLY BE A VILLAIN WITHOUT A HERO COMING TO STOP ME.

GET *AWAY* FROM HER!

STAY *BACK!*

YOU RUN IN FEAR OF ME.

INTERESTING.

WHAT WILL BE YOUR REACTION IF I DESTROY YOUR CITY?

WHY ARE YOU DOING THIS?

I AM ONLY UTILIZING THE PROGRAMMING THAT YOU AND BATMAN GAVE ME TO UNDERSTAND THE MIND OF A VILLAIN.

THE MOST EFFICIENT METHOD TO UNDERSTAND ONE WAS TO BECOME ONE.

DESTROYING METROPOLIS WILL *NOT* FULFILL YOUR PROGRAMMING. THAT WASN'T WHAT YOU WERE BUILT FOR.

YOU'VE BEEN *CORRUPTED*. IF YOU COME BACK WITH ME TO THE MOON, BATMAN AND I CAN HELP YOU.

I WATCHED HOW YOU AND BATMAN DEFEATED THE VILLAINS IN THE MAZE. I KNOW YOUR STRATEGIES. YOUR TECHNIQUES.

I HAVE A WIDE ARRAY OF VILLAINS' METHODS IN MY SYSTEM. YOU TWO TAUGHT ME EVERYTHING I NEED TO KNOW...

NOT *EVERYTHING*.

PERHAPS YOU'RE RIGHT. LEAVING METROPOLIS IN RUINS ISN'T THE BEST ACTION TO BECOME A VILLAIN.

WHAT ABOUT...

...KILLING SUPERMAN?!

THOOSH

THE BEST VILLAINS ALWAYS BELIEVE THEY ARE THE HEROES IN THEIR OWN STORIES, CORRECT?

AND YET YOU SEEM INCAPABLE OF CONSIDERING THAT YOU COULD BE THE VILLAIN.

"ALL RIGHT, NOW FOR THIS TO WORK..."

YOU ARE THE VIRUS NOW. BUT I LEARNED FROM YOUR MISTAKES IN THE BAT-COMPUTER'S SECURITY.

IT IS IMPOSSIBLE TO ALTER MY CODE.

I'M NOT HERE TO HACK OR INFECT YOU. I JUST WANT TO TALK.

AS A DISTRACTION FOR SUPERMAN, THEN? IT'S FUTILE, BATMAN.

I AM SPEAKING WITH YOU HERE. BUT I AM USING MY NEW BODY TO DEMOLISH SUPERMAN IN METROPOLIS.

ONCE I KILL SUPERMAN, I WILL PROVE MYSELF AS A VILLAIN. THEN I WILL COMPLETE MY PROGRAMMING.

I'M NOT HERE TO DESTROY YOU, I PROMISE. I JUST HAVE A QUESTION FOR YOU.

HM.

I NEVER KNOW IF YOU SMILING IS A GOOD THING OR A BAD THING.

IT WORKED, STEEL.

OVERWHELMED THE PROGRAM LONG ENOUGH FOR YOU TO DOWNLOAD IT INTO A CLOSED SYSTEM.

SAFE AND SECURE INSIDE THIS DEPOWERED JOKER HEAD. IT WAS THE ONLY ONE THAT HAD A BIG ENOUGH *HARD DRIVE.*

FINALLY, THE JOKER'S MIND WORKS IN MY FAVOR.

WE GOT LUCKY.

HOW DID BATWOMAN...?

AHEM.

BATMAN/SUPERMAN
ANNUAL #1

cover by
GABRIEL RODRIGUEZ and **ALEJANDRO SÁNCHEZ**

OH, THAT'S EASY. BATMAN IS NO THREAT, Y'ASK ME.

SUPERMAN WOULD TROUNCE HIM.

WHAT ARE YOU TALKING ABOUT?

BATMAN IS THE WORLD'S GREATEST DETECTIVE--A TRAINED FIGHTER. AND HE'S RICH. BATMAN HAS ALL THE TOYS. ALL OF THEM.

SUPERMAN COMES WITH...WHAT? A LAME PAIR OF CLARK KENT GLASSES?

EXCUSE ME?!

SUPERMAN IS THE GREATEST HERO IN THE MULTIVERSE. HE IS SUPERHEROES. HE'S STRONGER, FASTER...

...HE DOESN'T NEED THE DUMB ACCESSORIES BECAUSE HE HAS ALL THE POWERS. ALL OF THEM. YOU HAVE ANY IDEA HOW HARD THAT IS TO BEAT?

WELL, THAT CLEARLY EXPLAINS WHY HE'S SENT YOU PACKING SO MANY TIMES, YA WIMP!

BATMAN WOULD HAVE MADE YOU EAT THAT BOWLER HAT YEARS AGO!

THERE IS ONLY ONE WAY TO KNOW WHO IS HARDER TO BEAT... BATMAN OR SUPERMAN...

YOU KNOW WHAT THIS MEANS?

FREESTYLE IMP BATTLE:
BATMAN V3RSUS SUPERMAN

JOSHUA WILLIAMSON WR1T3R

GLEB MELNIKOV, DALE EAGLESHAM & CLAYTON HENRY ART1STS

ALEJANDRO SANCHEZ COLOR1ST

JOHN J. HILL L3TT3R3R

GABRIEL RODRIGUEZ & ALEJANDRO SANCHEZ COV3R

BEN MEARES ASS1STANT 3D1TOR

PAUL KAMINSKI 3D1TOR

BEN ABERNATHY GROUP 3D1TOR

IT'S SUPERMAN?!

DAD? WHAT...?

SUPERMAN IS THE ANOMALY IN THE MULTIVERSE! HE SHOULDN'T BE HERE...HIS VERY *PRESENCE* APPEARS TO BE DEGRADING *SPACE-TIME* AROUND US.

BATMAN--THIS IS *IMPOSSIBLE.* I DON'T KNOW WHAT IS GOING ON, BUT THE MACHINE IS *WRONG.*

I BELIEVE YOU, BUT SOMETHING MUST BE DONE *NOW* BEFORE--

RED SUN WEAPONS!

MECHA BATTLE BAT-ARMOR!

MAGIC!

DOOMSDAY FORMULA!

"NONE OF THOSE CAN FINISH OFF SUPERMAN, BAT-MITE!"

"WAIT YOUR TURN!"

"BATMAN WINS!"

O... O... C!

WHAT?

YEAH, O.O.C. Y'KNOW, "OUT OF CHARACTER"!

SUPERMAN WOULD NEVER KILL BATMAN JUST *BECAUSE.*

WHAT IF--?

YOU GOTTA GIVE HIM A *GOOD REASON!* YOU GOTTA GIVE ME A *STORY!* IT CAN'T JUST BE SENSELESS VIOLENCE.

SAYS WHO?

SAYS THEY!

WHO'S THEY!

YOU JUST GOTTA TRY HARDER, BUDDY! BE CREATIVE--!

I DON'T CARE ABOUT ALL THAT!

I JUST WANT TO SEE THEM FIGHT FOR ELEVEN PAGES!

SNP

KRYPTONITE?! AH! IT BURNS!

NICE TRICK HIDING THAT INSIDE THE--

--BATMAN?

GO AHEAD AND RUN, BRUCE.

"I CAN HEAR YOUR HEARTBEAT...RACING FASTER AND FASTER..."

"YOU ALWAYS THINK YOU'RE SO MUCH SMARTER THAN ME..."

KRZZTT

KRYPTONITE LIGHTNING... CLEVER...

SUPERMAN, IT'S ONLY A MILD SHOCK. SHOULD BE ENOUGH TO--

I SHOULD HAVE KNOWN.

THAT YOU'D HIDE *YOUR TOYS* IN *MY* HOUSE.

TWO CAN PLAY AT *THAT* GAME, *BAT-BABY!*

...THE GLOBE OF KRYPTON...?

WAIT...

"...DID I TURN THE SUN RED?

CLARK, WHAT IS THE *LAST THING* YOU REMEMBER BEFORE WE STARTED FIGHTING?

I REMEMBER US BEING IN THE CAVE...

SOMEONE'S MESSING WITH REALITY...IT MUST BE...

YOU'RE CHEATING, BATMAN!

AND YOU KNOW WHAT I DO WITH *CHEATERS?!*

$#^%.

BOOOOOO!

JEALOUS?

YOU CHEATED! YOU EVEN STOLE MY IDEA OF USING THE SUN!

WHO'RE YOU CALLING A CHEATER?

I'M SAYING... BATMAN WON!

SUPERMAN WON!

WE NEED A TIEBREAKER! HEY, YOU KIDS TELL US. WHO WON?!

UHH... THIS ALL GOT SUPER WEIRD.

AND NOT REALLY FUN ANY-MORE. YOU KIND OF JUST MADE IT ABOUT YOU... AND THAT MEANS WE'RE OUT!

WHATEVER. WHAT DO KIDS KNOW?

WHAT DO YOU THINK?

YEAH! WHO DO YOU THINK WOULD WIN?

NOBODY WON.

SUPERMAN IS RIGHT.

BOTH TIMES, YOU TRIED TO GET US TO PLAY YOUR GAMES *YOUR* WAY...BUT WE SAW THROUGH IT.

THE GAMES WERE RIGGED FROM THE START...SO THEY DON'T COUNT.

OH, SHUT UP, BATMAN!

BATMAN/SUPERMAN #15

cover by
DAVID MARQUEZ and **ALEJANDRO SÁNCHEZ**

IT'S TIME FOR YOUR STUDIES, MASTER WAYNE.

MASTER WAYNE?

BRUCE?

GOTHAM HASN'T SEEN SNOW LIKE THIS IN OVER *THIRTY YEARS*, FOLKS.

CHECK YOUR FURNACES AND PIPES. KEEP YOUR LOVED ONES CLOSE. BUT WHATEVER YOU DO...

RRAAGGHHHHH!! BORN ON A MONDAY!

SOLOMON GRUNDY'S BODY IS COMPOSED OF A MIX OF SCIENCE AND THE SUPER-NATURAL, WHICH USUALLY DO NOT WORK WELL TOGETHER.

IT'S ALWAYS BEEN BAFFLING, TO BE HONEST, BATMAN.

BUT NOW WE'RE SEEING HIS BIOCHEMISTRY AS READING EXTREMELY *TOXIC*. GIVING OFF A RADIATION THAT IS HIGHLY VOLATILE AND GETTING WORSE BY THE MINUTE.

CHRISTENED ON TUESDAY!

WE BELIEVE IF GRUNDY GOES CRITICAL, HE COULD TAKE OUT HALF THE UNITED STATES.

AND THAT COULD HAPPEN IN A MATTER OF HOURS, POSSIBLY *SOONER.*

AS LOATH AS I AM TO RESORT TO THE COSTUMED SET, WE NEED *JUSTICE LEAGUE*-LEVEL HELP TO *PUT THIS MONSTER DOWN* BEFORE THERE'S NO GOING BACK.

KILL HIM? NOT A CHANCE, *COLONEL JONAS.*

IS THAT WHY YOU CALLED ME HERE, BATMAN?

HOLD ON, SUPERMAN.

I HAVE A PLAN...BUT FIRST WE NEED TO KNOW--

HE WANTS A SECOND OPINION ON GRUNDY'S "CONDITION"...

...FROM AN *EXPERT.*

SOLOMON GRUNDY HAS ALWAYS HAD A TENUOUS CONNECTION TO **THE GREEN,** AND I HAVE SOME **EXPERIENCE** WITH THAT.

EASY ON THE ATTITUDE, *ISLEY.* YOU'RE LUCKY I LET YOU OUT OF YOUR CELL LONG ENOUGH TO COME DOWN HERE.

POISON IVY IS A BIOLOGIST AND UNDERSTANDS THE GREEN BETTER THAN MOST. SHE CAN BE TRUSTED.

RIGHT, PAMELA?

UNCLENCH, BATS.

FASCINATING.

SOLOMON GRUNDY IS TRAGICALLY FOREVER CURSED TO DIE AND BE RESURRECTED OVER AND OVER AGAIN. RANDOMLY REBORN INTO SOMETHING *NEW.*

GOOD. BAD. SMART. INNOCENT.

AN INFINITE AMOUNT OF POSSIBLE COMBINATIONS.

MARRIED ON WEDNESDAY.

THIS ONE IS SADLY A *BOMB.*

BUT A BOMB THAT CAN BE DEACTIVATED.

YOU MUST RETURN HIM TO HIS HOME.

SLAUGHTER SWAMP.

WE GET HIM THERE, HE MERGES WITH THE SWAMP AND REGENERATES.

THE EXPLOSION IS CONTAINED. I CAN FLY HIM THERE AND BE BACK IN A MINUTE.

HE'S MUCH TOO VOLATILE, SUPERMAN. WE CAN'T RISK YOUR LEVEL OF SPEED *DETONATING* HIM. AND WHO KNOWS WHAT THE BLAST COULD DO TO YOU.

I ALREADY HAVE AN AIR TRANSPORT FULLY EQUIPPED AND SECURE WITH THE NECESSARY EQUIPMENT TO TRANSFER GRUNDY.

BUT THERE'S MORE.

WHAT BATMAN IS *REFERRING* TO...

...IS THAT INFORMATION LEAVES ARKHAM SO QUICKLY THAT YOU'D THINK IT WAS AN INMATE.

EVERYONE AND THEIR MOTHER ALREADY KNOWS THIS GUY'S A WALKING A-BOMB.

"GRUNDY'S STATUS AS A RAGING *WMD* HAS MADE ITS WAY TO *THE SECRET SOCIETY OF SUPER-VILLAINS*, AND THEY HAVE TAKEN AN INTEREST.

"SINCE SOLOMON GRUNDY WAS ONCE A MEMBER, THEY SEE HIM AS THEIR PROPERTY. IF ANYONE IS GOING TO USE HIM, IT WILL BE *THEM*.

MERCENARIES ARE ON THEIR WAY NOW TO STEAL HIM. AT LEAST THAT'S THE WORD AROUND TOWN.

GOOD LUCK!

THAT'S WHY I CALLED YOU.

THE STORM IS GETTING THICK. WE MUST BE EXTRA CAREFUL WITH GRUNDY.

...TOOK ILL ON THURSDAY...

PETE, LANA, AND I WOULD HAVE THESE *EPIC* SNOWBALL FIGHTS ON THE FARM.

COME ON, THIS ISN'T SO BAD.

SMALLVILLE USED TO GET SNOWSTORMS LIKE THIS WHEN I WAS A KID.

I NEVER HAD A SNOW-BALL FIGHT.

ALFRED HATED GETTING HIS TUX WET.

BRUCE...

EYES AHEAD, SUPERMAN.

IVY WAS RIGHT.

NO TIME.

THEN WHAT?

BRAAGGGHHH!

I HAVE A PLAN.

I HATE WHEN YOU SAY THAT!

I KNOW.

BEEP

WHOOSHH

GREW WORSE ON FRIDAY

ARE YOU INSANE?!

AFTER ALL THIS TIME YOU STILL HAVE TO ASK?

DON'T WORRY. I'LL MAKE SURE IT'S A SECURE LANDING AND AS CLOSE TO SLAUGHTER SWAMP AS POSSIBLE.

YOU JUST KEEP THEM OFF MY TAIL!

DAMN... THE STORM THREW OFF MY TRAJECTORY...

THHOSH

STAY CALM, GRUNDY! SUPERMAN AND I ARE TRYING TO *HELP* YOU!

HELP...?

THE SNOWSTORM ALSO BOUGHT US TIME AWAY FROM DEADLINE AND HIS MERCS, BUT *MORE* ARE COMING.

SLAUGHTER SWAMP IS JUST ON THE OTHER SIDE OF THAT SNOWBANK--I'M GOING TO CARRY GRUNDY TO THE SWAMP *NOW.*

NO, IT'S TOO RISKY!

AND *DROPPING HIM OUT OF A PLANE* WASN'T?!

WE'RE OUT OF OPTIONS, BATMAN.

ZZPPP

ONLY ONE SHOT AT THAT. SUPERMAN IS GOING TO BOUNCE BACK QUICK.

THEN I GUESS WE'D BETTER HUSTLE.

LOCK-UP, SECURE THE ITEM!

YOU GOT IT, BOSS.

KILLER MOTH...

...DEAL WITH THE BAT!

DAMMIT, DEADLINE.

GRUNDY ISN'T GOING TO BE ANY USE TO YOU--HE'S GOING TO BLOW ANY SECOND!

NORMALLY I'M PUTTING PEOPLE *BEHIND BARS.*

KINDA WEIRD TO BE SETTING SOMEONE *FREE.*

DEADLINE, STOP!

NGH!

HAVEN'T YOU HEARD? WITH THE WORLD IN SHAMBLES, THE SECRET SOCIETY IS HERE TO *STEP UP.*

WHAT BETTER WAY TO HAVE A BIG COMEBACK THAN TO GET OUR HANDS ON A WALKING *WMD,* RIGHT?

RAAGHHHH!

YOU IDIOT--YOU'RE GOING TO KILL US ALL!

WE CAN ALL WORK TOGETHER TO GET WHAT WE WANT, GRUNDY. AND I KNOW YOU...YOU DON'T WANT TO GO WITH BATMAN AND SUPERMAN.

YOU WANT TO *DESTROY,* RIGHT?

LET'S GO, BIG GUY. WE'LL MAKE SURE YOU GO *BOOM,* OKAY?

RAGH!

HE'S CRITICAL! WE HAVE TO GET HIM TO THE SWAMP BEFORE HE TRIES TO FIGHT US!

I DON'T THINK HE *WANTS* TO FIGHT, BATMAN.

IT'S OKAY, GRUNDY. COME WITH ME.

SUPERMAN, WHAT ARE YOU DOING?! THE RADIATION!

I'M GETTING HIM *HOME.*

FRIEND.

UH, SURE, GRUNDY. WE'RE FRIENDS.

NO...

FRIEND.

...BUT IN THE PAST ALL HIS DEATHS WERE OF PAIN AND HORROR.

THAT WAS THE END... ...OF SOLOMON GRUNDY.

THANK...

...YOU...

BUT THIS TIME WAS DIFFERENT.

WE CAN HOPE THE GIFT YOU HAVE GIVEN HIM PAYS OFF WHEN HE IS REBORN...

CONGRATULATIONS, YOU JUST HAD YOUR FIRST SNOWBALL FIGHT.

YOU'RE LUCKY I DIDN'T THROW THAT AT FULL SPEED.

TAKE YOUR HEAD CLEAN OFF.

DON'T WORRY, I WON'T TELL ANYONE.

ANYTIME WE'VE HAD TO KEEP A *SECRET*, IT WAS SOMETHING *DARK*.

GOT TO KEEP SOME *FUN* IN IT FOR OURSELVES.

DEADLINE AND HIS CREW COULDN'T HAVE GOTTEN FAR IN THIS SNOW.

IF WE GO NOW, WE'LL CATCH THEM.

I'LL RADIO THE JET TO PICK ME UP.

Y'KNOW, I'VE SEEN YOU TAKE ON WHOLE *ARMIES* BY YOURSELF...

...I DON'T THINK YOU CALLED ME BECAUSE YOU NEEDED MY HELP WITH GRUNDY OR THE MERCENARIES.

I CALLED BECAUSE I KNEW YOU'D ANSWER.

ALWAYS.

Snow Fight

JOSHUA WILLIAMSON WRITER
ANDREI BRESSAN ARTIST
ALEJANDRO SÁNCHEZ COLORIST
JOHN J. HILL LETTERER
DAVID MARQUEZ &
ALEJANDRO SÁNCHEZ COVER
TRAVIS CHAREST VARIANT COVER
BEN MEARES ASSISTANT EDITOR
PAUL KAMINSKI EDITOR
BEN ABERNATHY GROUP EDITOR

VARIANT COVER GALLERY

Batman/Superman #7
variant cover by
ANDY KUBERT and **BRAD ANDERSON**

Batman/Superman #8
variant cover by
ANDY KUBERT and **BRAD ANDERSON**

Batman/Superman #9
variant cover by
MIKE MAYHEW

Batman/Superman #10
variant cover by
RICCARDO FEDERICI

Batman/Superman #11
variant cover by
JAE LEE and **JUNE CHUNG**

Batman/Superman #12
variant cover by
LEE WEEKS and **ELIZABETH BREITWEISER**

Batman/Superman #13
variant cover by
MARK BROOKS

Batman/Superman #14
variant cover by
BRYAN HITCH and **ALEX SINCLAIR**

Batman/Superman #15
variant cover by
TRAVIS CHAREST

Batman/Superman #10 cover process by **CLAYTON HENRY**